ARROYO CENTER

T0097343

Defense Planning in a Time of Conflict

A Comparative Analysis of the 2001–2014 Quadrennial Defense Reviews, and Implications for the Army— Executive Summary

Eric V. Larson, Derek Eaton, Michael E. Linick, John E. Peters,
Agnes Gereben Schaefer, Keith Walters, Stephanie Young,
H. G. Massey, Michelle Darrah Ziegler

Prepared for the United States Army

For more information on this publication, visit www.rand.org/t/rr1309z1

Library of Congress Cataloging-in-Publication Data is available for this publication.

ISBN 978-0-8330-9975-4

Published by the RAND Corporation, Santa Monica, Calif.

© Copyright 2018 RAND Corporation

RAND® is a registered trademark.

Support RAND
Make a tax-deductible charitable contribution at
www.rand.org/giving/contribute

www.rand.org

Preface

The RAND Arroyo Center conducted a study for the U.S. Army titled Defense Planning in a Decade of Conflict. The purpose of the project was to perform a comparative historical review of the four Quadrennial Defense Reviews (QDRs) conducted since the first QDR in 1997—including QDR reports in September 2001, February 2006, February 2010, and March 2014—to identify larger trends, as well as implications and recommendations for the Army to shape the conduct of and thereby improve future reviews.[1]

The main product of that project was a report—*Defense Planning in a Time of Conflict: A Comparative Analysis of the 2001–2014 Quadrennial Defense Reviews, and Implications for the Army*—that documented the results of our analysis to Army and Department of Defense senior leaders and planners well enough in advance that measures can be taken now to improve the organization, processes, and analytics associated with the next Defense Strategy Review.[2] This report provides a stand-alone Executive Summary that captures the key findings and recommendations of the larger report. Both the main report and the Executive Summary may be of interest to defense planners in the U.S. Army, Office of the Secretary of Defense, and Joint Staff, as well as students of defense planning in the scholarly community.

This research was sponsored by the Office of the Deputy Chief of Staff, G-3/5/7, and conducted within the RAND Arroyo Center's Strategy, Doctrine, and Resources Program. RAND Arroyo Center, part of the RAND Corporation, is a federally funded research and development center sponsored by the United States Army.

The Project Unique Identification Code (PUIC) for the project that produced this document is HQD146687.

---

[1] An earlier study assessed the three major defense planning exercises following the end of the Cold War. See Eric V. Larson, David T. Orletsky, and Kristin J. Leuschner, *Defense Planning in a Decade of Change: Lessons from the Base Force, Bottom-Up Review, and Quadrennial Defense Review*, Santa Monica, Calif.: RAND Corporation, MR-1387-AF, 2001.

[2] See Eric V. Larson, Derek Eaton, Michael E. Linick, John E. Peters, Agnes Gereben Schaefer, Keith Walters, Stephanie Young, H. G. Massey, and Michelle Darrah Ziegler, *Defense Planning in a Time of Conflict: A Comparative Analysis of the 2001–2014 Quadrennial Defense Reviews, and Implications for the Army*, Santa Monica, Calif.: RAND Corporation, RR-1309-A, 2018.

Contents

Figures and Tables

Figures

Tables

Acknowledgments

We would like to thank Daniel Klippstein, deputy director of Strategy, Plans and Policy, Headquarters, Department of the Army G-35 SS, for sponsoring our study, as well as COL Jeff Hannon, Headquarters, Department of the Army G-35 SSP, who served as action officer for the study. We also wish to thank Tim Muchmore, Headquarters, Department of the Army G-8, QDR, for his support of our study.

Achieving the study's goals required an in-depth understanding of the four Quadrennial Defense Reviews from the perspective of participants in the reviews. Accordingly, the authors would like to gratefully acknowledge the assistance of the many defense professionals who agreed to participate in structured conversations about their participation in and perspectives on the conduct of the Quadrennial Defense Reviews. As they were promised anonymity, these individuals must remain nameless.

We wish to express our gratitude to RAND colleagues Richard Darilek and Burgess Laird and to our external reviewer, GEN Walter L. Sharp, U.S. Army (Ret.), for their very helpful reviews.

We also would like to thank RAND colleagues Michael Johnson for his early advice and other assistance on this project, Josh Klimas for his assistance with data on Army force structure changes, Robert Leonard and Akesha James for data from Selected Acquisition Reports, and Irina Danescu for her expert assistance in finalizing the data on force structure and Army global posture over time. We also wish to thank Donna Mead, Angela Grant Clayton, and David Richardson for their administrative support in the preparation of this report.

We also wish to thank Terence Kelly, director, Strategy, Doctrine, and Resources research program, Arroyo Center; Bruce Held, former deputy director, Arroyo Center; and Timothy Bonds, director, Arroyo Center for their support and assistance over the course of this study. Finally, we would like to thank the Army Fellows class of fiscal year 2015 for their comments on a briefing in which we previewed emerging findings from the study.

We have benefited greatly from the assistance provided by all of these individuals. Errors of fact or interpretation, of course, remain the authors' responsibility.

Abbreviations

9/11	September 11, 2001, terrorist attacks
BCT	brigade combat team
CJCS	Chairman of the Joint Chiefs of Staff
DoD	U.S. Department of Defense
FY	fiscal year
FYDP	Future Years Defense Program
GWOT	global war on terrorism
OCO	overseas contingency operations
OSD	Office of the Secretary of Defense
OUSD	Office of the Under Secretary of Defense
QDR	Quadrennial Defense Review
WMD	weapons of mass destruction

Introduction

The National Defense Authorization Act for fiscal year (FY) 1997 established the requirement for the U.S. Department of Defense (DoD) to conduct a Quadrennial Defense Review (QDR) and report the results of that review (in a QDR report) by May 1997. The statutory language associated with producing the report was subsequently amended to synchronize its release with the President's budget submission the year following the review. As amended, the statutory language that existed in early 2014 called for the report to address a broad array of 17 distinct issues.

The QDR is one of a number of statutorily required strategy reports, including the following:

- *Annual National Security Strategy report.* A National Security Strategy report is to be produced within 150 days of an administration entering office, with subsequent annual reports submitted simultaneously with each new President's budget.[1] As will be described, however, neither the George W. Bush administration nor the Barack Obama administration met the 150-day requirement or the requirement for annual reports after its first such report.
- *Biennial review of National Military Strategy.* Not later than February 15 of each even-numbered year, the Chairman of the Joint Chiefs of Staff (CJCS) shall submit a report containing the results of a comprehensive examination of the national military strategy consistent with the most recent National Security Strategy and Quadrennial Defense Review.[2]

In addition, although there is no statutory requirement for doing so, DoD periodically produces a National Defense Strategy to support the Planning, Programming, Budgeting, and Execution process.[3] That process presumes that a National Defense

---

[1]   United States Code, Title 50, Section 3043, Annual National Security Strategy Report, 2013.

[2]   United States Code, Title 10, Section 153, Chairman: Functions, 2010.

[3]   After the conduct of this research, the National Defense Authorization Act for FY 2017 established a requirement for a National Defense Strategy while dropping a formal requirement for a Defense Strategy Review. References in this document to a "Defense Strategy Review" should be construed as referring to the collection of analytic activities conducted to create a National Defense Strategy.

Strategy will establish the plans for military force structure, force modernization, business processes, supporting infrastructure, and required resources (funding and manpower) and that the report will provide a link between the National Security Strategy and the National Military Strategy. There is no statutory requirement for a National Defense Strategy outside the provision for the QDR.

Since the results of the first QDR were published by the Bill Clinton administration in May 1997,[4] subsequent QDR reports have been published by the Bush administration in September 2001[5] and February 2006[6] and by the Obama administration in February 2010[7] and March 2014.[8]

Objectives and Approach

The Office of the Deputy Chief of Staff, G-3/5/7, asked researchers at the RAND Arroyo Center to provide a systematic comparative assessment of the QDR reports conducted in the Bush and Obama years, over a period of nearly a decade and a half of conflict in Afghanistan, Iraq, and elsewhere. The intent of the assessment was to provide Army strategists and planners, as well as others, with a DoD-wide picture of the development, contents, and implementation of decisions taken in each QDR, while highlighting the U.S. Army's experience during and as a result of each review. The assessment also aimed to identify key lessons and offer recommendations to the Army and DoD for improving the organization, processes, and outcomes of future defense reviews. The analysis yielded a final report—*Defense Planning in a Time of Conflict: A Comparative Analysis of the 2001–2014 Quadrennial Defense Reviews, and Implications for the Army.*[9] This document represents a stand-alone Executive Summary of the larger report.

For the assessment, we conducted an interdisciplinary analysis built on a mix of mutually reinforcing analytic efforts, which included the following:

- *Analysis of official documents.* We conducted a detailed review of each QDR report produced between 2001 and 2014, as well as other publicly available information,

---

[4]   DoD, *Report of the Quadrennial Defense Review*, Washington, D.C., May 1997.

[5]   DoD, *Quadrennial Defense Review Report*, Washington, D.C., September 30, 2001.

[6]   DoD, *Quadrennial Defense Review Report*, Washington, D.C., February 6, 2006.

[7]   DoD, *Quadrennial Defense Review Report*, Washington, D.C., February 2010.

[8]   DoD, *Quadrennial Defense Review Report*, Washington, D.C., March 2014a.

[9]   Eric V. Larson, Derek Eaton, Michael E. Linick, John E. Peters, Agnes Gereben Schaefer, Keith Walters, Stephanie Young, H. G. Massey, and Michelle Darrah Ziegler, *Defense Planning in a Time of Conflict: A Comparative Analysis of the 2001–2014 Quadrennial Defense Reviews, and Implications for the Army*, Santa Monica, Calif.: RAND Corporation, RR-1309-A, 2018.

including DoD press briefings, news releases, interviews, congressional hearings, annual budget requests, posture reports, manpower requirements reports, modernization and other planning documents, Selected Acquisition Reports, QDR Terms of Reference, and other available official sources.

- *Budget analysis.* We spent considerable effort analyzing budget documents to develop a budget database that would enable us to separately assess base budget spending and spending on overseas contingency operations (OCO) by service and appropriation title.
- *Secondary analysis of other official assessments.* We also reviewed assessments of the QDRs, the budget plans that implemented them, and of various issues relevant to each QDR, including assessments from the U.S. Government Accountability Office, the Congressional Budget Office, the Congressional Research Service, internal memoranda, and press reporting.
- *Structured conversations.* Finally, to gain a better understanding of the key issues, dynamics, and debates associated with the development of each QDR, we developed a protocol for conducting structured conversations with more than a dozen individuals who were involved in some capacity with each QDR, either in the Office of the Secretary of Defense (OSD), the Joint Staff, or Headquarters, Department of the Army.

This Executive Summary presents an overview of our results in examining each of the four QDRs—2001, 2006, 2010, and 2014—and then examines some key trends that draw across all four reviews. It ends with a discussion of our overall conclusions and recommendations.

Overview of Assessments of the 2001, 2006, 2010, and 2014 Quadrennial Defense Reviews

In providing an overview of our assessments of the QDRs between 2001 and 2014, we focus on each review's organization and process, strategy development, force planning, resources, risk assessment, and reception. Our assessment also details between-QDR changes in each of these dimensions of defense planning so that readers can better understand and appreciate the multiplicity of other forces at work in shaping the defense strategy, program, and resources.

2001 Quadrennial Defense Review

Organization and Process

The 2001 QDR formally began in June 2001, following confirmation of senior civilian leaders and completion of several external study panels that Secretary of Defense Donald Rumsfeld had commissioned to advise him. The QDR did not build on the foundation of a new National Security Strategy because such a strategy would not be available until 2002. The late start left only a little more than three months to meet the September 30, 2001, reporting deadline. Much of the work had been finalized before the September 11, 2001, terrorist attacks (9/11), but the review reportedly underwent some modest revisions thereafter.

The 2001 QDR demonstrates the unpredictability and turbulence in defense planning that can emerge as a result of the transition to a new administration. For example, Army and other preparations for the QDR that were undertaken in 2000 (during the Clinton administration) seem to have been nearly irrelevant to the efforts of Secretary Rumsfeld and the new OSD team. The result was that Army QDR activities were essentially put on hold during the first half of 2001, and the Army was then faced with the requirement to adapt to emerging guidance while also defending end strength and force structure. It is unclear whether the Army could have foreseen or hedged against any of these developments.

In any event, in December 2002, OSD promulgated DoD Directive 8260.1, *Data Collection, Development, and Management in Support of Strategic Analysis*, which established policy and assigned responsibilities for the generation, collection, development, maintenance, and dissemination of data on current and future U.S. and non-U.S. forces in support of DoD strategic analyses, such as the QDR. However, these efforts to standardize analytical baselines, scenarios, and other analysis elements would not come to their full fruition until the establishment of the "Analytic Agenda" after the 2006 QDR.[1]

Strategy Development

The 2001 QDR report was the first strategy document of the Bush administration. As such, it generally disregarded the outgoing Clinton administration's December 2000 National Security Strategy and was developed without the benefit of an equivalent statement from the new administration.

Force Planning

The force-planning construct developed in the 2001 QDR went well beyond the two-nearly-simultaneous-wars construct that had prevailed since 1993—for example, by including the homeland defense mission. However, the authors of the QDR do not appear to have fully reckoned the military personnel requirements associated with the final "1" in the "1-4-2-1" force-planning construct—described in the QDR as "decisively defeating" an adversary, which most took to mean regime change. This points to a weakness in the QDR process in estimating the military personnel requirements of executing the national defense and military strategies at low to moderate risk.

Analyses of the military capabilities required to execute the defense strategy and meet the demands implied by the 1-4-2-1 force-planning construct at low to moderate risk led us to judge that existing force structure and end strength were sufficient, and assessments of future capabilities that adversaries might present suggested that transformation goals could be accomplished by focusing on key segments of the force.

For the Army, the preservation of force structure and end strength in the 2001 QDR represented a qualified success, even though the demands of Afghanistan and Iraq ultimately raised questions about the sufficiency of Army capabilities and capacity to conduct stability operations following regime change in Iraq. Force structure and end strength remained relatively stable over the FY03–06 implementation period, although in January 2004, Secretary Rumsfeld approved, on an emergency basis, a waiver to increase active Army end strength above authorized levels by 30,000 personnel to better meet operational demands. The Army, somewhat remarkably, was also able to begin transforming its operational force from division-based organizations to

---

[1]   For the evolution of DoD efforts to establish Support for Strategic Analysis, see DoD, *Data Collection, Development, and Management in Support of Strategic Analysis*, Washington, D.C., DoD Directive 8260.1, December 6, 2002; DoD, *Support for Strategic Analysis*, Washington, D.C., DoD Directive 8260.01, January 11, 2007; DoD, *Support for Strategic Analysis (SSA)*, Washington, D.C., DOD Directive 8260.05, July 7, 2011; and Jason Sherman, "Work Grabs Reins Of Analysis Effort Pivotal To Strategy, Budget Decisions," *Inside Defense*, November 26, 2014.

modular organizations based on brigade combat teams, even as it conducted operations in Afghanistan and Iraq.[2]

Risk Assessment

The 2001 QDR report proposed a powerful way of thinking about risk that would influence the next two QDRs as well. However, this key contribution—the risk assessment framework—was not fully operationalized, either during or after the conduct of the 2001 QDR. And although Secretary Rumsfeld's preoccupation with uncertainty and surprise found expression in the QDR report, a key assumption of the review— that the United States was in a period in which it could safely engage in development of future capabilities while accepting some risk in current capabilities—was essentially shattered by the 9/11 attacks. At that point, any consideration of end strength and force structure cuts ended and transformation took a back seat to the more immediate operational challenges associated with the war in Afghanistan, and soon thereafter, the war in Iraq.

Resources

The 2001 QDR aimed to repair the problems that had emerged as a result of inadequate defense resources during the previous administration. It also aimed to put DoD on a new course that emphasized transformation of the force, capabilities-based planning to better address uncertain future threats and challenges, and further reform of DoD business practices. The Future Years Defense Program (FYDP) was never explicitly linked to the QDR initiatives, thus breaking the connection between the two. As a result of 9/11 and the wars in Afghanistan and Iraq, resources during the period were relatively unconstrained. Such generous budgets and supplemental appropriations that were provided after 9/11 enabled DoD to simultaneously conduct two major contingency operations in Afghanistan (beginning in October 2001) and Iraq (beginning in March 2003); conduct a variety of smaller operations related to what was at the time called the global war on terrorism (GWOT); and promote Secretary Rumsfeld's transformation agenda. Preexisting DoD challenges in managing defense resources were compounded by the somewhat ambiguous rules about what sorts of expenditures were appropriate for the base budget and GWOT funding.

Reception

The 2001 QDR was widely praised for its efforts to focus DoD on potential future adversary capabilities and on transformation efforts to better address them. In the end,

---

[2] A 2004 report suggested that modularization would necessitate more than 100,000 structural changes to the Army. Then–Chief of Staff of the Army Peter Shoomaker described the enormity of the modularization as follows: "This is the biggest internal restructuring we've done in 50 years, but it must be done to make us relevant and to allow us to meet the real threat to the United States" (see Jim Garamone, "Army Chief 'Adamantly Opposes' Added End Strength," *American Forces Press Service*, January 28, 2004).

the Army judged its performance in the 2001 QDR to have been a qualified success: Many of the Army's recommendations were incorporated into the QDR, and, despite the strained relations with OSD and the general contentiousness of the process, the Army was able to avoid large-scale cuts to its force structure and budget.

All told, the principal contributions of the 2001 QDR arguably were threefold: its arguments for the necessary resources to restore the health of the force; its introduction of a longer-term perspective on defense planning and greater efforts to transform U.S. military forces; and its introduction of a sophisticated risk assessment framework that focused attention on not just operational risk but also force management risk, institutional risk, and, perhaps most important, future challenges risk.

2006 Quadrennial Defense Review

Organization and Process

The 2006 QDR was an "evolutionary, not revolutionary" report that updated the thinking expressed in the 2001 QDR to deal with a wider range of threats while continuing DoD transformation efforts. The QDR also built on the September 2002 National Security Strategy, drafts of an updated National Security Strategy that would be released the month after the QDR report, the May 2004 National Military Strategy, and the March 2005 National Defense Strategy.

Although preliminary work on the QDR began in late 2004, the formal kickoff occurred with the release of the Terms of Reference in early March 2005. Because the statutory language for the QDR was amended after the 2001 edition, the deadline for the next QDR was February 2006 so that the report would be released at the same time as the President's budget request for FY07.

While some level of confusion and turbulence is apparent in the development of all the QDRs we reviewed, participants found this to be particularly so for the 2006 QDR, partly because of its exceedingly complex organization (six panels and 26 subgroups) and efforts to run it as a "rolling QDR" that would generate decisions over the course of its conduct, among other reasons. Thus, after the QDR's conclusion, OSD, the Joint Staff, and the services began collaborative work on developing what came to be called the "Analytic Agenda": an agreed-upon set of principles, scenarios, models, and data that would facilitate analytic cooperation and transparency in results.

Strategy Development

Rather than introducing a new strategy, the QDR essentially embraced the recently released March 2005 National Defense Strategy. Four focus areas from the QDR's strategy—defeat terror, defend homeland, shape choices, and prevent weapons of mass destruction (WMD)—were used to guide development of the review's force-planning construct, dubbed the "Michelin Man," by which planners hoped to refine the earlier construct and make it more relevant to the post-9/11 security environment. Their approach to doing this was to focus on the military steady-state and surge requirements of three mission areas—homeland defense, irregular warfare/GWOT, and conventional campaigns. The 2006 QDR cast the military as an agent for shaping the following key domains:

1. defeating terrorist networks
2. defending the homeland in depth
3. shaping choices of countries at strategic crossroads
4. preventing the acquisition or use of WMD.

In terms of force structure, the QDR arguably had the greatest effect on special operations forces, which were to be substantially increased.

Force Planning

With the "Michelin Man," the QDR refined the "1-4-2-1" force-planning construct to adapt it to the post-9/11 security environment and make it more suitable for consideration of homeland defense, irregular warfare (especially the GWOT), and conventional campaigns. This new construct also prescribed a capability for two nearly simultaneous conventional campaigns—or one conventional campaign and one large-scale, long-duration irregular campaign. Thus, the 2006 QDR report demonstrated a greater recognition of Army and other ground force requirements for irregular warfare than had the 2001 QDR.

Ultimately, the QDR reported that the size of the force was about right, although it also directed an increase in special operations forces formations. On force structure, the QDR reported that the size of the force was about right, although it also directed an increase in special operations forces and their formations. Although the QDR did not conduct a detailed analysis of end-strength requirements, it endorsed the existing and planned permanent active Army end strength level of 482,400, while proposing an increase in special operations forces, as well as long-term reductions to conventional U.S. ground forces following completion of action in Afghanistan and Iraq. By the fall of 2006, however, it had become clear that active Army and Marine Corps end strength levels were too low, and an increase was needed. Thus, the QDR failed to anticipate ground force personnel requirements, leading to Secretary of Defense Robert Gates's decision in January 2007 to increase permanent Army and Marine Corps active-duty end strength by 92,000 personnel.

Risk Assessment

The QDR relied on a refined version of the risk assessment framework and, with analyses from a Joint Staff effort dubbed *Operational Availability-06*, appears to have strengthened its analytic basis for conducting risk assessments.

Resources

The FY07 President's budget that was submitted along with the QDR focused new investments on "leading-edge" elements proposed in the QDR, with the expectation that those investments would continue to be implemented in FY08, FY09, and thereafter. Importantly, the FY07 budget also would support increases in Army combat power and further ground force modernization through the Future Combat System. Budgets continued to be generous over the implementation period for the QDR, and distinctions between what could be paid for with base budget funding and what could be paid for with GWOT funding remained somewhat vague.

Reception

The reception to the QDR was somewhat mixed, with the principal criticism being that it was a "budget-driven exercise" that failed to meet the requirements of the statute for an unconstrained analysis of strategy and force requirements. House Armed Services Committee Chairman Duncan Hunter went so far as to conduct his own committee review of defense strategy.

Much remained to be done after the 2006 QDR report and the FY07 budget request to flesh out the directions set in the QDR, including the completion of more than 140 follow-on actions, the development of nine major roadmaps, and the development of the FY08 and subsequent budgets that were to do the heavy lifting in implementing the thinking in the QDR through programmatic and budgetary actions. Notwithstanding the 2006 QDR report's failure to anticipate the force-structure requirements of Iraq and Afghanistan, its endorsement of a permanent post-war active Army end strength of 482,400 soldiers represented another qualified success for the Army.

2010 Quadrennial Defense Review

Organization and Process

Although the 2010 QDR was the first QDR of the new Obama administration, the continuation of Robert Gates as Defense Secretary appears to have introduced greater continuity and stability than likely would otherwise have been the case. Although informal work on the QDR began earlier, the formal kickoff was in late April 2009. Most of the detailed analyses were reportedly done by five issue teams that reported through Deputy Assistant Secretary of Defense David Ochmanek to Undersecretary of Defense for Policy Michele Flournoy, and to the Deputy Secretary and Secretary. The conduct of the QDR appears to have benefited greatly from the Analytic Agenda, which helped OSD, the Joint Staff, and the services ensure that their analyses would be transparent to one another. Specifically, our research suggests that the Analytic Agenda contributed to a much smoother process in the 2010 QDR. The development of the Analytic Agenda appears to have facilitated broader understanding, reduced miscommunication, and fostered transparency and trust among participants, and it could serve as a model for laying the foundation for future QDRs.

Strategy Development

While the 2010 QDR was the first formal strategy statement of the new Obama administration—a new National Security Strategy was in draft form but would not be published until May 2010, three months after the release of the QDR, and a new National Military Strategy would not be released until February 2011—it did not entirely represent a clean break from the earlier administration's strategic thinking. The QDR's strategy built on the June 2008 National Defense Strategy, the January 2009 Quadrennial Roles and Missions Review Report (both conducted under Secretary Gates during his service in the Bush administration), and Gates's January 2009 article, "A Balanced Strategy."[3]

The 2010 QDR was the first truly "wartime QDR." It gave primacy to securing favorable outcomes in Afghanistan and Iraq, as well as rebalancing the current force, rather than preparing for longer-term threats. This was summarized well in the tenets of the QDR's defense strategy—prevailing in today's wars, preventing and deterring conflict, preparing to defeat adversaries and succeeding in a wide range of contingencies, and preserving and enhancing the all-volunteer force—and by CJCS Michael Mullen's top three priorities: winning today's fight, balancing global strategic risk, and enhancing the health of the force.[4]

Therefore, the 2010 QDR report's strategy shifted the focus of defense planners' attention from the sorts of longer-term threats and challenges that had preoccupied the authors of the 2001 and 2006 QDRs to the requirements associated with the sorts of irregular wars then being conducted in Iraq and Afghanistan, while also considering a broader range and combination of threat scenarios. Our Army interlocutors viewed this shift to ground force requirements as highly favorable to the Army.

Force Planning

In light of the increased complexities of defense planning, Secretary Gates reportedly eschewed the development of a simple "bumper sticker" force-planning construct. But the QDR's four stated priorities provide a sense of the demands the force-planning construct aimed to address: prevail in the ongoing U.S. military operations; ensure a defense in depth of the United States, preventing the emergence or reemergence of transnational terrorist threats and deterring other potential major adversaries; prepare

---

[3]   Robert M. Gates, "A Balanced Strategy: Reprogramming the Pentagon for a New Age," *Foreign Affairs*, January/February 2009.

[4]   See the statement of Vice Adm. P. Stephen Stanley, U.S. Navy, Director for Force Structure, Resources, and Assessment, J-8, Joint Staff, in U.S. House of Representatives, *The 2010 Quadrennial Defense Review: Hearing Before the Committee on Armed Services*, Washington, D.C., February 4, 2010, p. 7.

for significant new challenges; and preserve and enhance the all-volunteer force. The force-planning construct used in the 2010 QDR reportedly flowed from the 2006 QDR's "Michelin Man" construct to multiple *integrated security constructs*—that is, different combinations of scenarios that the force needed to be capable of managing. From an Army perspective, the greater focus on the irregular warfare and counterinsurgency requirements of Iraq and Afghanistan in the QDR 2010 were quite welcome.

In terms of manpower, the QDR enshrined earlier decisions to increase permanent Army and Marine Corps end strength to meet the demands of the wars in Afghanistan and Iraq. Army end strength reportedly was not an issue in the 2010 QDR; it was understood that the service could afford the structure that was funded in the previous FYDPs. Moreover, the Army had been on a path to grow, as it was clear that it was under significant stress. In 2009, Secretary Gates authorized a temporary end-strength increase of 22,000 active-component soldiers to further mitigate growing manpower shortages in deploying units.

Risk Assessment

The risk assessment framework developed in the 2001 QDR continued to be the touchstone for the risk assessment in the 2010 QDR. The 2010 framework was updated to add a fifth category of risk: strategic, military, and political risk.

Resources

The financial crisis of 2008–2009 had pushed the United States into a Great Recession by the time of the 2010 QDR, cutting gross domestic product growth and revenues and increasing unemployment. But according to our structured conversations, there was not much discussion in the 2010 QDR about what the longer-term fiscal environment might look like. Indeed, the proposed defense budget for FY11 reflected real growth in defense spending for the foreseeable future. Although it was not yet clear at the time, the year the QDR was released also marked the apex of defense spending.

Still, earlier increases in end strength and planned increases in base spending levels over the FY11–15 FYDP gave DoD additional resources in support of President Obama's decision to conduct a "surge" in Afghanistan, even as combat troops were withdrawing from Iraq.

Reception

A number of criticisms were levied at the 2010 QDR, including the following:

- By taking a short-term (five- to seven-year) focus on the conflicts at hand, the QDR was shorting preparations for future conflict.
- The QDR understated the military requirements for deterring and defeating challenges from state actors while simultaneously overestimating the capabilities of the force.

- There were difficulties in ascertaining the QDR's priorities for different contingencies or mission types.
- There was a lack of clarity in the force-planning construct.
- There was an absence of significant changes to planned force structure.
- There was a lack of clarity about future capability gaps.
- There were fighter and ship funding and acquisition shortfalls, even as the strategy increasingly emphasized these capabilities.
- Cuts in research, development, test, and evaluation spending had an impact on longer-term capabilities and transformation.

In turn, DoD officials publicly defended the QDR.

The 2010 QDR arguably represented an unqualified success for the Army: The QDR's focus on meeting near-term warfighting requirements and its endorsement of the earlier decisions to increase permanent active Army end strength were highly favorable to the Army.

2014 Quadrennial Defense Review

Organization and Process

The 2014 QDR was a transitional defense review that aimed to guide DoD from a period dominated by wartime operations to one that would be better able to address emerging threats. The QDR focused on the period following the end of major U.S. involvement in OCO in Afghanistan and Iraq and the resetting of the force. As a result, the QDR report also was an evolutionary document that built on the February 2010 QDR, the May 2010 National Security Strategy, the January 2012 Defense Strategic Guidance, and the July 2013 Strategic Choices and Management Review. The Defense Strategic Guidance established the defense strategy, identified which missions would be used to size military capabilities and capacity, and determined that U.S. forces would no longer be sized to conduct large-scale, prolonged stability operations like the ones that had been conducted in Afghanistan and Iraq. For its part, the Strategic Choices and Management Review identified options for reshaping the force and DoD institutions under three budget cut scenarios, and it identified the resources that would be needed to support the defense strategy and its force requirements.

The 2014 QDR development process was very short, only about five months, beginning after the Strategic Choices and Management Review was completed and concluding in March 2014. This was, in part, because the basic defense strategy had already been set in the February 2010 QDR and refined in the January 2012 Defense Strategic Guidance, and resource requirements and funding options had been vetted by the Strategic Choices and Management Review. Thus, much of the work of the QDR lay in refining concepts that were developed earlier.[5]

Finally, whereas the development of the Defense Strategic Guidance reportedly had been a relatively open process, the development of the 2014 QDR was largely the work of the most-senior-level civilian and military leaders. In the end, the 2014 QDR report essentially became a vehicle for formally codifying, cementing, and explaining to internal and external audiences the decisions that had been taken in the Defense Strategic Guidance and Strategic Choices and Management Review in a statutorily required QDR report.

Perhaps in response to the difficulties encountered in the 2014 QDR, in a July 2014 memorandum, the service vice chiefs reportedly recommended strengthening the Support for Strategic Analysis (i.e., Analytic Agenda) process, which generates baselines, scenarios, and concepts of operation that support high-level deliberations on defense strategy, weapon system programming and budget matters, force sizing, and capability development. In November 2014, it was reported that, acting on the vice chiefs' recommendation, Deputy Secretary Robert Work announced plans to reinvigorate the Support for Strategic Analysis process.[6] Thus, there is some hope that the Defense Strategy Review of 2017–2018 might benefit from the sort of transparent and collaborative process associated with the Analytic Agenda in the 2010 QDR.

Strategy Development

In his cover letter to the QDR, Secretary of Defense Chuck Hagel noted that the 2014 review built on the 2012 Defense Strategic Guidance and gave priority to "three strategic pillars": defending the homeland, building security globally, and remaining prepared to win decisively against any adversary. The Secretary also noted the imperative to "rebalance the military over the next decade and put it on a sustainable path to protect and advance U.S. interests and sustain U.S. global leadership."[7] The steps Secretary Hagel proposed to reach a sustainable path included "making much-needed reforms across the defense enterprise. We will prioritize combat power by reducing unnecessary overhead and streamlining activities. . . . [We] must reform military compensation."[8]

The review was also informed by the knowledge that the United States had concluded combat operations in Iraq and that operations in Afghanistan might also conclude in the near term, especially given the difficulties the United States faced in arriving at the status of forces agreement with the Karzai government that was required to make continued operations possible.

---

[5] For example, according to our structured conversations, there was significant attention to the question of how to refine the definitions and interpretations of *defeat* and *deny* that had been embraced in the strategy.

[6] See Sherman, 2014.

[7] DoD, 2014a, p. i.

[8] DoD, 2014a, p. i.

The authors of the QDR appeared willing to accept some additional risk in executing the strategy at their proposed budget levels, but they warned of more-severe consequences for defense should DoD face sequestration spending levels that would require further cuts in modernization, readiness, and other accounts.

Force Planning

To assist in planning the FY19 force structure, the 2014 QDR assessed the capacity of the force to manage several different combinations of scenarios (that is, the integrated security constructs), which constituted the QDR's force-planning construct. The 2014 QDR summarized its force-structure goals and force-planning construct as seeking

> forces, in aggregate, [that] will be capable of simultaneously defending the homeland; conducting sustained, distributed counterterrorist operations; and in multiple regions, deterring aggression and assuring allies through forward presence and engagement. If deterrence fails at any given time, U.S. forces could defeat a regional adversary in a large-scale multi-phased campaign, and deny the objectives of—or impose unacceptable costs on—another aggressor in another region.[9]

With a more aggressive Russia, a more assertive China, the rise of the Islamic State in Iraq and Syria, a still-active al-Qa'ida network, the requirement to leave a residual force of perhaps 10,000 personnel in Afghanistan to train Afghan security forces and keep the Taliban at bay, capability shortfalls for combating WMD, and such emerging challenges as cyber threats, achievement of U.S. national objectives in the current strategic environment almost certainly appears more demanding than the environment the nation faced prior to the attacks of September 11, 2001.[10]

In the 2014 QDR, the Army was directed to provide 440,000–450,000 active-duty personnel, 195,000 U.S. Army Reserve personnel, and 335,000 Army National Guard personnel. These reduced levels reflected an acceptance of additional risk in executing the defense strategy in order to meet the constraints imposed by the new, more-stringent budgets. Special operations forces personnel were increased.

Given that the United States and potential adversaries have both increased their capabilities over the years, it is somewhat difficult to find fault with the National Defense Panel's position that the current environment requires a force that is at least as large as the 1993 Bottom-Up Review's planned force that was essentially in place before 9/11. For the Army, this is perhaps 480,000–490,000 active-duty personnel, substantially higher than the currently envisioned range of 420,000–450,000.

---

[9] DoD, 2014a, p. 22.

[10] For an analysis of the ground-force requirements associated with WMD elimination operations, see Timothy M. Bonds, Eric V. Larson, Derek Eaton, and Richard E. Darilek, *Strategy-Policy Mismatch: How the U.S. Army Can Help Close Gaps in Countering Weapons of Mass Destruction*, Santa Monica, Calif.: RAND Corporation, RR-541-RC, 2014.

Risk Assessment

Although the analytics were never fully developed, the 2001, 2006, and 2010 QDRs benefited from a strong risk assessment framework that focused attention on operational, force management, institutional, and, perhaps most importantly, future challenges risks. The 2014 QDR dispensed with the risk assessment framework that had been a mainstay of those QDRs and instead relied on a new risk assessment framework that had been developed by CJCS Martin Dempsey.

The Chairman's assessment of risk identified three main areas of higher risk: the capacity of the QDR-directed force to defend the homeland while conducting simultaneous high- to mid-intensity defeat and deny campaigns; the low probability that reductions in U.S. capacity could be completely offset by an increased reliance on U.S. partners; and the assumed risk in the capacity of each service, particularly ground forces. The Chairman described the risks associated with sequestration-level funding in much starker terms.

While the Chairman's risk assessment in the 2014 QDR report used a framework that was arguably more explicitly tied to the National Security Strategy, it lacked an explicit emphasis on addressing longer-term threats and challenges through the development of transformational military capabilities or through the ability to make trade-offs among operational, force management, institutional, and future challenges risks. Nor did it address a new category of risk that had emerged since the 2010 QDR: resources risk, arising from uncertainty about budgets and the prospect that budgets will be inadequate to ensure low to moderate levels of risk in executing the defense strategy. While the new framework may prove useful in the near term for the Chairman's annual risk assessment, whether the framework will prove equally valuable for longer-term planning against future threats and challenges remains to be seen.

Resources

The 2014 QDR was conducted in the shadow of the Budget Control Act and the sequestration-driven cuts that were to result from that legislation. Secretary Hagel described the 2014 QDR as "neither budget driven nor budget blind,"[11] and indeed, this QDR was more resource-conscious than previous defense reviews. Unlike previous QDR reports, the 2014 QDR report discussed strategic requirements alongside resourcing requirements and risks, and it included an entire chapter on implications of further budget reductions. Thus, the report was described by its authors as being "strategy-driven, but resource-informed."[12] The Strategic Choices and Management

---

[11]   DoD, "News Release: DoD Releases Fiscal 2015 Budget Proposal and 2014 QDR," Washington, D.C., March 4, 2014b.

[12]   See the testimony of Deputy Under Secretary of Defense Christine Wormuth in U.S. House of Representatives, *The 2014 Quadrennial Defense Review: Hearing Before the Committee on Armed Services*, Washington, D.C., April 3, 2014.

Review concluded that the 2012 Defense Strategic Guidance could not be executed under the Budget Control Act and sequestration. Because that guidance had not been written to accommodate the cuts mandated by sequestration, the 2014 QDR needed to address issues of strategy in light of the new fiscal constraints.

However, although there seemed to be agreement among the administration, the independent National Defense Panel, and many members of Congress that sequestration-level funding would have a crippling effect on the nation's defenses and that more resources were needed, the budget plan for FY15 provided only sequestration-level funding while failing to authorize defense reform measures that would yield the most savings.

Accordingly, it appeared highly likely that some sort of congressional action would be taken in 2015 to provide defense with additional resources. It was unclear what form this action might take—reliance on OCO accounts to fund base budget activities, a reprise of the Balanced Budget Act of 2013 scheme of providing a year of relief, a revision to the caps to preserve defense and cut domestic spending, or, less likely, outright repeal of sequestration. Still, additional action to bolster defense funding appeared all but inevitable.

Reception

House Armed Services Committee Chairman Howard P. "Buck" McKeon immediately rejected the QDR, saying that the document was heavily constrained by low budget levels rather than identifying the budget levels that would ensure low to moderate risk in executing the strategy. Chairman McKeon also called for DoD to resubmit a new QDR.[13]

From the Army's standpoint, there was not really any one thing in the Defense Strategic Guidance, Strategic Choices and Management Review, or QDR guidance that the Army could not do. Rather, the Army argued that there was not a low- to moderate-risk way to do all of them—or even to be prepared to do all of them—in combination. No service chief or secretary wants to be put in the position of limiting options available to the President in response to a crisis. But the projected arc of Army readiness, modernization, and force structure would create a situation in which every decision on how to use the Army would result in a discussion about what contingent options would be closed down by that decision. The scope of contingent options that would be closed down was assessed as creating a high risk to the ability to meet the demands of the strategy.

---

[13] House Armed Services Committee, "Chairman McKeon Rejects QDR," press release, Washington, D.C., March 4, 2014.

Main Trends

In this section, we summarize the major trends we observed in the four QDRs across the categories presented: organization and process, strategy development, force planning, risk assessment, resources, and reception.

Organization and Process

Although there are some important points of continuity across the organizations and processes for the QDRs addressed in this executive summary, each QDR differs in its organizational and procedural details.

Each QDR appears to have enjoyed the involvement of senior civilian and military leaders, including the Secretary of Defense, Deputy Secretary of Defense, Chairman and Vice Chairman of the Joint Chiefs of Staff, service secretaries and chiefs, and Under Secretary of Defense for Policy; in addition, the combatant commanders were brought in at key points throughout the process.[1] Decisionmaking groups at the secretary and deputy secretary levels were supported by between five and eight working-level groups (depending on the QDR) and, in the case of the 2006 QDR, more than two dozen subgroups. There also appears little doubt that the 2010 QDR benefited from the continued service of Secretary Gates, who had been in office since 2006 and offered additional continuity during the first QDR of the Obama administration. Because the OSD and Joint Staff organization and process for QDRs are somewhat in a class by themselves, the Army has generally had to wait until these structures were in place to effectively organize itself to support them.

In terms of process, in all cases, informal work on the QDRs by OSD, the Joint Staff, and the services began well before the formal kickoff of the QDR. For the 2010 QDR, which benefited from agreement on an Analytic Agenda after the 2006 QDR, this preparatory work paid off handsomely. But for the 2001 QDR, when the Joint Staff was sidelined during much of the preliminary effort, their early work made a

---

[1] That said, we found very little information on the role that Secretary Hagel played in the development of the 2014 QDR.

less consequential contribution to QDR deliberations. Somewhat uniquely, the 2014 QDR was conducted based on an already specified strategy (the January 2012 Defense Strategic Guidance), as well as an assessment of resources (the August 2013 Strategic Choices and Management Review). The Analytic Agenda in the 2010 QDR, which was a reaction to the somewhat confusing 2006 QDR process, also may have contributed to a somewhat smoother process at the working level—although, during the end game of that review, there were harried efforts to pare it down. More impressionistically, the somewhat grand aims that are used to describe the ambitions for the QDRs at the beginning of the process have tended to give way to more-realistic and more-limited aims at the end.

A final key finding from an organizational and process perspective is the nearly unanimous view that the Analytic Agenda that was developed after the 2006 QDR paid tremendous dividends in the 2010 QDR in terms of the clarity and transparency of various stakeholders' positions and analysis. We believe that many of our interlocutors would endorse Deputy Secretary Robert Work's decision in November 2014 to reinvigorate the Support for Strategic Analysis process so that the next Defense Strategy Review might benefit from the sort of analytic infrastructure that the Analytic Agenda represented, as well as from the collaborative analytic community that formed around it.

Strategy Development

Although most planners would envision a top-down strategy development process that begins with a National Security Strategy and subsequently derives a National Defense Strategy and National Military Strategy, the historical record shows a different pattern (see Figure 1).

As shown in the figure, neither the Bush nor the Obama administration submitted its first National Security Strategy before the release of its first QDR, and neither preceded its second QDR with an updated National Security Strategy. The order of release of National Defense Strategy and National Military Strategy reports shows a similar lack of orderly, top-down, strategy development. Thus, the Bush and Obama periods demonstrate the essentially chaotic nature of strategy development; moreover, there is little reason at present to believe that this is likely to change with the 2018 Defense Strategy Review.

That said, although they have accented different themes and used different frameworks to portray their strategic logic, there has been significant continuity in the basic national security, defense, and military strategies described in the past four QDR reports (see Table 1).

Figure 1
Release of Defense Strategy Documents, 2001–2015

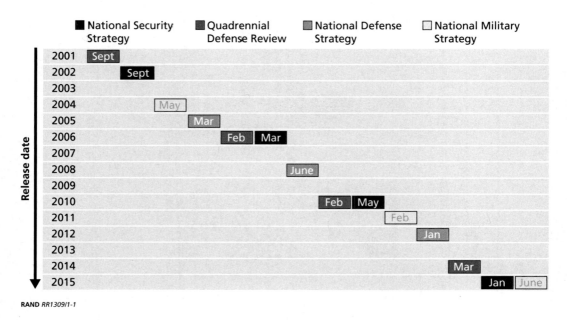

RAND RR1309/1-1

Force Planning

Notably, each QDR aimed to provide military support to homeland defense activities, while attempting to preserve, in one fashion or another, a capacity to conduct two overlapping, large-scale military campaigns (a staple of post–Cold War defense planning, as shown in Table 2), as well as supporting some number of additional operations, including smaller-scale contingencies.

Table 1
QDR Strategy Elements, 2001–2014

Strategy Element	2001 QDR	2006 QDR	2010 QDR	2014 QDR
National interests and objectives	• Ensure U.S. security and freedom of action • Honor international commitments • Contribute to economic well-being	• No explicit discussion of U.S. national interests	• Strengthen and maintain the integrity and resiliency of an international system that promotes security, prosperity, a broad respect for universal values, and an environment conducive to cooperative action	• Prioritize U.S. security and that of allies and partners • Promote a strong economy in an open economic system • Respect universal values • Support an international order that promotes peace, security, and opportunity through cooperation
Defense policy goals	• Assure allies and friends • Dissuade future military competition • Deter threats and coercion against U.S. interests • If deterrence fails, decisively defeat any adversary	• Defeat terrorist networks • Defend the homeland • Shape the choices of countries at strategic crossroads • Prevent hostile actors from acquiring and using WMD	• Rebalance capabilities to prevail in current wars while building the capability to deal with future threats • Prevent and deter conflict • Prepare to defeat adversaries and succeed in a wide range of contingencies • Preserve and enhance the all-volunteer force • Reform DoD to better support the urgent needs of the warfighter, buy weapons that are affordable and truly needed, and ensure that taxpayers' money is not wasted	• Rebalance to the Asia-Pacific region • Maintain a strong commitment to Europe and the Middle East • Sustain a global approach to countering violent extremists and terrorist threats • Continue to protect and prioritize key investments in technology while our forces overall grow smaller and leaner • Invigorate efforts to build innovative partnerships and strengthen key alliances and partnerships

Table 1—Continued

Strategy Element	2001 QDR	2006 QDR	2010 QDR	2014 QDR
Strategic environment	• United States in asymmetrically advantageous position • Pervasive uncertainty regarding future threats	• Nation involved in a long war against terror (U.S. operations successful in key areas of Afghanistan and Iraq) • Geographic isolation no longer provides security to the United States • Continuous change and reassessment required to defeat "highly" adaptive enemies • Possible emergence of a hostile major power with high-end military capabilities	• Current fight is the top priority • United States will remain the most powerful actor, but will increasingly rely on key allies and partners to sustain stability and peace • U.S. interests and role in the world require armed forces with unmatched capabilities, as well as a willingness on the part of the nation to employ them in defense of its interests and the common good	• Changes (geopolitical, nature of modern war, fiscal) in the security environment require a rebalancing of the force • A period of fiscal austerity and an uncertain future fiscal environment • Rapidly changing security environment • No more large-scale counter-insurgency or stability operations
Key trends	• Rapid advancement of military technologies • Increasing proliferation of CBRNE weapons and ballistic missiles • Emergence of new areas of military competition (space and cyber) • Increasing potential for miscalculation and surprise	• Broadly similar to the 2001 QDR	• Rise of China and India will shape the international system in ways not easily defined • Diffusion of global economic, military, and political power • Increasing influence and capability of nonstate actors • Proliferation of WMD	• Possibility that China's growth and rapid military modernization may increase risk of regional conflict • Increasingly contested air, sea, space, and cyberspace domains • Increasing ease with which sophisticated WMD can proliferate • Climate change

SOURCE: RAND analysis of DoD 2001, 2006, 2010, and 2014a.

NOTE: CBRNE = chemical, biological, radiological, nuclear, and enhanced high-explosive.

Table 2
DoD Force-Planning Constructs, 1993–2014

	1993 Bottom-Up Review	1997 QDR	2001 QDR	2006 QDR	2010 QDR	2014 QDR
Force-planning construct	2 major regional conflicts	2 major theater wars	1-4-2-1	Refined wartime construct: the "Michelin Man"	Not stated	Not stated
Major elements	Defeat 2 regional threats nearly simultaneously	Defeat large-scale, cross-border aggression in 2 theaters in overlapping timeframes + Smaller-scale contingencies	Homeland defense + Deter aggression in 4 critical theaters + 2 swift defeats (win 1 decisively)	Homeland defense + 2 conventional contingencies or 1 conventional + 1 irregular warfare contingency	Homeland consequence management events + 2 large-scale land campaigns or 1 large air/naval campaign + 1 campaign in 2nd theater or 1 large land campaign + 1 long-term irregular warfare campaign	Homeland defense, provide support to civil authorities + 1 full combined-arms campaign across all domains + Deny objectives or impose unacceptable costs on 2nd opportunistic aggressor
Focus	Size for 2 major regional contingencies, other contingencies are lesser-included cases	Size for 2 major-theater wars plus steady-state smaller-scale contingencies; swing some forces to 2nd major conflict	Emphasize forward defense; focus on four priority theaters; accept risk in a 2nd major conflict	Shift capabilities to address 4 focus areas and long-duration irregular warfare; address steady-state and surge demand	Address size, as well as shape; address multiple-scenario cases for the near and long terms; address surge and steady-state demand, including long-term irregular warfare	Do not size the force for large and protracted stability operations; rebalance to the Asia-Pacific region; maintain reversibility as an option

Table 2—Continued

	1993 Bottom-Up Review	1997 QDR	2001 QDR	2006 QDR	2010 QDR	2014 QDR
Context	Gulf War; demand for a peace dividend; deficit reduction	Bosnia; peace dividend; transformation	Transform the force; support the GWOT	Long war; change capabilities mix; force is sized about right	Support for OCO funding and defense budget cuts	Post-war and sequestration-era budgets and force-structure cuts; preparation for future challenges

SOURCE: RAND analysis and Gunzinger, 2013, pp. 19–20.

Force Structure

As suggested by Table 3, there were changes both to the size and shape of the force over the years reviewed.

Table 3
General-Purpose Force Structure, FYs 2001–2015

Service Element	FY01	FY06	FY10	FY14[a]	FY15[b]
Army					
Divisions (AC/RC)	10/8	10/8	10/8	10/8	10/8
Maneuver brigades (AC)[c]	36	35	45	38	32
Maneuver battalions (AC)[d]	106	137	141	152	128
Navy					
Aircraft carriers	12	12	11	10	10
Carrier air wings (AC)	10	10	10	10	10
Attack submarines	55	54	53	54	54
Surface combatants	108	101	112	99	93
Marine Corps					
Divisions (AC/RC)	3/1	3/1	3/1	3/1	3/1
Expeditionary forces	3	3	3	3	3
Air wings (AC/RC)	3/1	3/1	3/1	3/1	3/1
Air Force					
Fighter squadrons (AC/RC)[e]	46/38	45/38	36/35	33/27	29/29
Bombers (AC)	130	118	123	111	112
Special Operations Forces					
Military manpower[f]	41,785	49,086	47,878	63,263	63,141

SOURCE: Office of the Under Secretary of Defense (OUSD) (Comptroller), "DoD Budget Request," web page, various years, *Operation and Maintenance Programs (O-1)* and Operation and Maintenance supporting volumes of each service; OUSD (Comptroller), *National Defense Budget Estimates for FY 2015*, Washington, D.C., April 2014.

NOTE: AC = active component; RC = reserve component.

[a] These figures depict FY14 enacted budget data from OUSD (Comptroller), 2014.

[b] These figures depict FY15 proposed force structure in OUSD (Comptroller), 2014.

[c] Starting with the FY08/09 budget, the Army used brigade combat teams (BCTs) as its base force-structure accounting measurement. In prior years' budgets, the Army listed the number of battalions by type. Actual maneuver brigade figures for FY99 through FY06 are derived from division force structure of the appropriate year plus nondivisional maneuver brigades and regiments, such as the 173rd Airborne Brigade (now an airborne interim BCT), 170th Infantry Brigade (deactivated in FY12), 172nd Infantry Brigade (deactivated in FY13), 194th Armor Brigade (deactivated as a maneuver brigade in FY05), 3rd Armored Cavalry Regiment (Stryker BCT since FY12), and 2nd Armored Cavalry Regiment (Stryker BCT since FY05).

[d] For the purpose of this study, a *maneuver battalion* is any infantry battalion, armor battalion, cavalry squadron, or combined arms battalion of the various mutations of maneuver brigades that have been part of Army force structure since 2001. Actual maneuver battalion figures for FYs 99–06 account for all active-component infantry and armor battalions and cavalry squadrons. For FYs 07–14, with

Table 3—Continued

modularity complete for all active-component BCTs (with the exception of two remaining legacy brigades), we derived the actual maneuver battalion from modular BCT force structure, which includes two infantry battalions and one light cavalry squadron in interim BCTs, two combined arms battalions and one armored reconnaissance squadron in armored BCTs, and three infantry battalions and one cavalry squadron in Stryker BCTs. By FY14, most BCTs had assumed the Army 2020 Table of Organization and Equipment framework, which included a third maneuver battalion in interim BCT and armored BCT structure.

e For FYs 99–05, we use the squadron numbers reported in the Operation and Maintenance supporting volumes of the active Air Force, Air National Guard, and Air Force Reserve budget submissions. For FY06 forward, we estimate the number of squadrons in the active and reserve components based on the number of reported primary aircraft authorized and the observed ratio of aircraft to squadrons from FYs 99–05. The ratios are as follows: 22 aircraft per F-15 and, later, F-22 squadron; 12 aircraft per A-10 squadron; 20 aircraft per F-16 squadron; and 18 aircraft per F-117 squadron. Budget data from FYs 01–07 also yielded the ratio of aircraft per squadron for the reserve component: 12 aircraft per Air National Guard A-10 squadron; 15 aircraft per Air Force Reserve A-10 squadron, and 15 aircraft per fighter (F-15 and F-16) squadron in both the Air National Guard and Air Force Reserve.

f These figures include Military Department Major Force Program 11 activities only.

While retaining ten active-component and eight reserve-component division flags, the Army transformed its force structure into more highly deployable modular BCTs; these peaked in number over the 2010–2013 period.[2] Meanwhile, as other major naval force elements remained relatively stable, the number of naval surface combatants also peaked and then dropped well below the initial 2001 levels. Air Force fighter squadrons fell significantly over the period, while special operations forces grew in a dramatic fashion.

Manpower and End Strength
The wars in Afghanistan and Iraq created significant demands for U.S. military forces, especially ground forces. Figure 2 portrays the number of in-country troops in Afghanistan and Iraq in October of every year from 2002 to 2014.[3] As shown in the figure, the total number of personnel peaked in 2007 at nearly 190,000.

---

2   Some reorganization also was taking place over FY14 and FY15 that moved battalions from eliminated brigade combat teams to construct other three-battalion teams.

3   The number does not include combat support and combat service support personnel in the region.

Figure 2
In-Country U.S. Troop Levels in Afghanistan and Iraq, 2002–2014

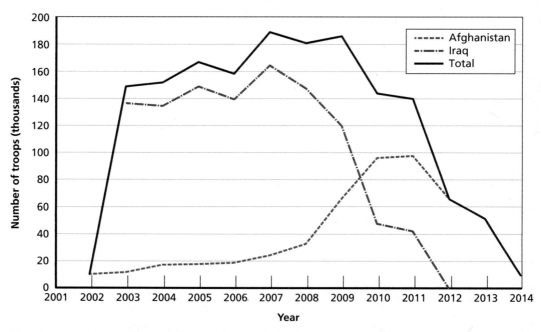

SOURCE: Amy Belasco, *The Cost of Iraq, Afghanistan, and Other Global War on Terror Operations Since 9/11*, Washington, D.C.: Congressional Research Service, December 8, 2014, Appendix A.
RAND *RR1309/1-2*

Figure 3 portrays active Army end strength from 2001 to 2015. As shown in the figure, the Army began the period with about 480,000 personnel in active-duty end strength in FY01 and saw only modest growth until the permanent end-strength increase announced by Secretary Gates in January 2007. Thereafter, end strength peaked in FY10 and FY11 at 566,000 personnel and was estimated to be 490,000 in FY15.

It is also notable that key manpower-related decisions were taken off-cycle; that is, they occurred between QDRs. Active Army end-strength increases occurred in early 2004, early 2007, and mid-2009, for example, while decisions to undertake "surges" in Afghanistan and Iraq were announced in January 2007 (Iraq) and December 2009 (Afghanistan).

Figure 3
Active Army End Strength, FYs 2001–2015

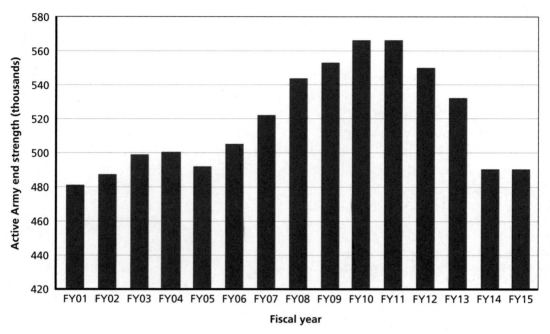

SOURCE: OUSD (Comptroller), 2014, Table 7-5.
RAND *RR1309/1-3*

Risk Assessment

Although the analytics were never fully implemented by OSD and although the Chairman and Joint Staff never fully embraced it, the risk assessment framework developed in the 2001 QDR—which focused attention on operational, force management, institutional, and future challenges risks—had a surprisingly lasting influence on subsequent QDRs. It was not until the 2014 QDR that the framework appears to have fallen out of favor. And the Chairman's risk assessment in the 2014 QDR report lacked the explicit emphasis on addressing longer-term threats and challenges, and it did not consider resources risk.

Another common theme across all the QDRs examined was that the Chairman's risk assessment of the strategy presented in the QDR was always stated as being contingent on the availability of resources, which were never actually specified in the QDR.

Resources

Each QDR was influenced by the nation's economic and budgetary outlook at the time. The 2001 QDR was conducted when the outlook was quite positive, and the 2006 QDR was conducted during a period of relatively strong economic growth. The 2010 QDR was conducted in the wake of the financial crisis of 2008–2009, and the 2014 QDR was conducted under the shadow of sequestration. Because the government never raised taxes to pay for the wars, they were financed through deficit spending.

Defense budgets grew dramatically over 2001–2014. As shown in Figure 4, DoD budget authority, including both the base budget and GWOT or OCO spending, peaked over FYs 08–10 at the highest levels seen since 1948—a period that included wars in Korea and Vietnam, as well as the Ronald Reagan administration buildup of the 1980s.

Figure 4
DoD Budget Authority, FYs 1948–2019

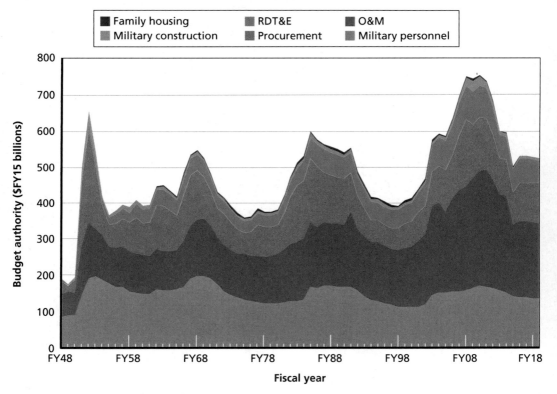

SOURCE: RAND analysis of OUSD (Comptroller), 2014, Table 6-8.
NOTES: Because OCO funding is financed on an annual basis, totals after FY14 reflect only planned base budget discretionary spending and do not include OCO funding. O&M = operation and maintenance.
RAND *RR1309/1-4*

Nonetheless, although QDR themes and priorities have frequently been high-lighted in post-QDR budget presentations and have led to some major initiatives, we conclude that the chain of causality linking QDR guidance and directives with the detailed elements of defense programs and budgets developed after a QDR is often opaque, or at best indirect. While additional efforts to establish more-direct and more-explicit links could improve the transparency of defense strategy, programs, and budgets, real-world events can still render QDR priorities obsolete. For example, the 9/11 attacks and the post-invasion counterinsurgency demands of Iraq reduced DoD's latitude to promote the 2001 QDR's transformation agenda, and the Defense Strategic Guidance released five months after the Budget Control Act of 2011 significantly revised defense strategy less than two years after the release of the 2010 QDR report.

Reception

A consistent response from members of Congress and the independent panels that reviewed the QDRs was concern that proposed forces might be inadequate to meet the demands of the strategy and that proposed resources might be insufficient to support the force structure. Another criticism was that the QDRs failed to take a long-term (20-year) view of national security challenges and defense needs, looking no further out than the current FYDP. In addition, the QDRs were criticized for not addressing all the subjects specified in enabling legislation, although it is not clear that the expansive list of mandated topics could ever be covered in a QDR. Most notably, perhaps, this list included identifying the resources required to support the strategy. Many observers viewed the QDRs as highly resource-constrained rather than as documents that illuminated the true resource requirements of the proposed defense strategy and programs.

Recommendations and Conclusions

The QDRs of 2001 through 2014 each, in their own way, wrestled with the emerging national security and military threats and challenges and sought to provide strategic and other guidance on the future development of U.S. military capacity and capabilities. Assessing the implications of these reviews for defense programs, force structure, end strength, and budgets is greatly complicated by the wars that were conducted over this period, the combination of annual defense budget requests and supplemental appropriations, and the somewhat elastic boundaries between base budget and OCO spending. Nonetheless, we offer some observations and recommendations that may improve the conduct of future Defense Strategy Reviews.

Value, Timing, Organization, and Process

We conclude that the principal value of QDRs is the opportunity that they present to codify DoD senior leadership's thinking about defense strategy and priorities within the Department and communicate this thinking to Congress, the American public, friends, and adversaries. The first QDR of a new administration also has some value in signaling departures from the strategic thinking of the previous administration.

Our research suggests that the disorderly timing of the release of key strategy reports may be further complicating an already complicated QDR process. Neither the Bush nor the Obama administration produced a National Security Strategy report within the statutorily mandated deadline of 150 days after taking office, making the 2001 and 2010 QDRs the first formal, publicly available strategic statements of each administration. To provide a firmer foundation for service contributions to the QDR and for the CJCS's development of a new National Military Strategy, we believe that the value of an administration's first QDR (or, rather, given the new statutory language, Defense Strategy Review) might be enhanced if a new National Security Strategy report was in fact published within 150 days of entering office, or released simultaneously with each Defense Strategy Review.

- *Recommendation*: DoD and the White House should consult with Congress on the current statutorily mandated deadlines for producing the National Security Strategy and Defense Strategy Review reports and consider whether a different schedule would better ensure that a new National Security Strategy either precedes or accompanies Defense Strategy Review.

Given the complexity of the analytics and the range of stakeholders who need to be involved in QDRs, complex organizations and processes seem unavoidable, and the short timelines for concluding QDRs have frequently led administrations to narrow scope and involvement as deadlines approach. Although DoD efforts to improve the Support for Strategic Analysis process began in 2002, the unwieldy and confusing organization associated with the 2006 QDR probably undermined any resulting gains from these efforts, and the benefits of what came to be called the Analytic Agenda were not fully realized until the 2010 QDR. Although the Analytic Agenda fell into disrepair after that, recent DoD efforts to revive the Support for Strategic Analysis process offer some promise in helping to standardize future QDR organizations and analytic processes. And although Army organizations and processes in the QDRs appear to have worked well, our research suggests that personalities, leadership styles, and the cultivation of good professional working relationships at all levels may have mattered more.

- *Recommendation*: Develop a cadre of senior Army staff who have experience and contacts in OSD and the Joint Staff, intimate knowledge of how the system works, and credibility outside the Army, and involve these individuals in future Defense Strategy Reviews.

Our research shows that force-planning constructs were adapted over the various QDRs to better address an increasingly rich portfolio of threats and challenges that required forces and capability development. However, only the 2010 QDR's constructs explicitly included the steady-state requirements of planned or potential smaller-scale contingency operations, or the potentially large ground force requirements for WMD elimination operations, both of which could be important future considerations for defense planning.

- *Recommendation*: Efforts should continue to consider a greater range and combination of mission types in the development of scenarios for assessing the next force-planning construct. In particular, much greater attention to the requirements of WMD elimination and other counter-WMD missions appear especially warranted, and these missions arguably should be promoted to the first rank of missions that drive force requirements. In addition, the ongoing steady-state requirements of smaller-scale contingency operations, and the challenges of disengaging from these operations to meet emerging threats, should be considered more explicitly in future defense reviews.

- *Recommendation*: Although the complexity of force planning in today's environment may militate against simplistic "bumper sticker" force-planning constructs, one that might help to better address the growing portfolio of demands on the force would be to adapt the 2001 QDR's force-planning construct into a "1-4-2-1-n." This construct would be capable of ensuring homeland defense, deterring aggression and coercion in four key regions, conducting two major campaigns of various types (including a conventional campaign that includes WMD elimination operations of the kind that might be encountered in North Korea), achieving decisive victory (regime change) in one of these campaigns, and sustaining current ongoing smaller-scale contingency operations.

Analytics

On the analytics of QDRs, our structured conversations brought to our attention the contributions of the Analytic Agenda that was developed between the 2006 and 2010 QDRs. That agenda resulted in an agreed-upon set of defense planning scenarios, models, and data that helped to ensure that OSD, the Joint Staff, and the services had a common analytical picture while conducting the 2010 QDR. We believe that the revival of the Analytic Agenda in the form of the Support for Strategic Analysis process could greatly facilitate collaborative planning, improve transparency, and reduce misunderstanding in future Defense Strategy Reviews.

- *Recommendation*: Promote and shape the DoD-wide effort to reinvigorate the Support for Strategic Analysis process (including the organizational arrangements and processes) and common analytic resources that can support the next Defense Strategy Review, and press to institutionalize these elements within DoD so that they are available during the conduct of future reviews.
- *Recommendation*: Serve as a thought leader regarding how the Army fits into future joint campaigns, while improving the Army's ability to conduct analyses of ground-force requirements in these future campaigns.
- *Recommendation*: As part of the effort on where the Army fits into future joint campaigns, develop new scenarios that could stress ground and joint force capacity and capabilities in key emerging mission areas. A scenario detailing a WMD elimination operation as part of a larger joint campaign in North Korea would be ideal for inclusion in the next Defense Strategy Review. Additional consideration of the steady-state rotational requirements of various numbers and combinations of smaller-scale contingencies also would be worthwhile.

Our structured conversations suggest that the Army analytic community is widely viewed within DoD as possessing the greatest expertise for assessing the ground-force requirements associated with conventional ground campaigns, and that, while the

Army's Total Army Analysis process has improved over the period to consider non-conventional mission areas and the generating force, critiques of that process suggest that the techniques and tools for assessing the requirements for other-than-conventional ground-force missions and the generating force are underdeveloped. The credibility of Army analyses of other missions is accordingly not yet as high as it is for conventional missions.

- *Recommendation*: The Army should review its analytic capabilities and capacity to assess the full range of missions that are of contemporary concern; identify shortfalls and gaps that impede its ability to conduct equally credible assessments of nonconventional missions and the generating force; and identify doctrinal, organizational, training, materiel, leadership and education, personnel, and facility changes that will improve its analytic ability to address this fuller set of missions.

Further developing the Army's analytic capabilities for assessing force structure and manpower requirements and risk assessments in nonconventional mission areas (and the generating force) will help to improve the analytic transparency of Army arguments, so that they are better understood by the OSD and Joint Staff analytic communities, while demonstrating that Army positions rest on clean analytic arguments. Doing so facilitates socialization of Army positions and improves the overall persuasiveness of Army arguments.

Indeed, our structured conversations suggested that the Army needs to be heavily engaged with OSD and the Joint Staff to socialize these external audiences to Army issues and analyses well before the kickoff of any future Defense Strategy Reviews. The conversations also revealed a number of opportunities for doing so, including Program Objective Memorandum guidance, annual program budget reviews, and the requirements process, not to mention less-formal vehicles, such as briefings, workshops, and conferences.

- *Recommendation*: In anticipation of the next Defense Strategy Review, consider creating additional informal mechanisms for discussing issues related to the Army and ground forces with OSD and the Joint Staff, to better socialize them to emerging issues and analytic results.

Risk Assessments

As noted in our analysis of the 2001 QDR, in many ways, the risk assessments conducted by OSD and the CJCS lie at the heart of the QDR process; this is where assessments of ends, ways, and means take place, and where judgments about the ability of the force to execute the defense strategy are made. Moreover, the estimated risk in executing the defense strategy also is one of the bottom-line topics of greatest interest to Congress.

The 2001 QDR introduced a sophisticated risk assessment framework that focused on operational risk, force management risk, institutional risk, and future challenges risk. This framework also was employed in the 2006 QDR and, with the addition of strategic, military, and political risks, in the 2010 QDR. Nonetheless, the analytic underpinnings of that framework were never fully developed, and it was not used in the 2014 QDR.

- *Recommendation*: The Army, OSD, and the Joint Staff should review, refine, and build out the analytics of the 2001 QDR risk framework and, in connection with reinvigorating the Support for Strategic Analysis process, develop the necessary analytic underpinnings to assess with greater fidelity the level of risk associated with different force, end-strength, and resource levels.

In addition to the failure of the QDRs' force-planning constructs to capture the full range of operational demands on the force, issues related to end strength and the active-reserve mix were largely unexamined in the QDRs from 2001 to 2014. Our historical review suggests a recurring tendency toward a peacetime requirement for 480,000 or more active Army personnel:

- In 2001, prior to 9/11, the active Army had 480,000 active personnel.
- The 2006 QDR called for a post-war Army of 482,400, which was the permanent end-strength level at the time.
- The post-QDR plan in 2010 was to return active Army end strength to 482,400.
- The FY13 budget following the release of the Defense Strategic Guidance called for 490,000 active Army personnel.
- In 2014, the National Defense Panel endorsed a comparable number.

Yet the Army is currently on a path to 440,00–450,000—an end-strength level that Chief of Staff of the Army Raymond T. Odierno has described as "an absolute floor" that already accepts higher risk in some areas[1]—or possibly even an active end strength of 420,000.

The argument that the Army may not have the end strength to be able to execute the defense strategy at low to moderate risk is a powerful and compelling one. The key challenge for the Army will lie in its ability to generate credible, transparent, and persuasive estimates of the types and levels of risk associated with the 490,000, 440,000–450,000, and 420,000 active end-strength forces and their associated budgets.

---

[1] Raymond T. Odierno, "Total Force Policy for the U.S. Army," statement before the Senate Armed Services Committee, Washington, D.C., April 8, 2014.

- *Recommendation*: As the service most reliant on manpower, the Army should continue to refine its capabilities for assessing the risk associated with different end strengths and mixes of active-component and reserve-component forces and press for fuller consideration of these issues in the 2018 Defense Strategy Review.
- *Recommendation*: It will be important in the next Defense Strategy Review for the Army to provide additional assessments of the active end strength that is required to support the defense strategy, as well as the risks that are being accepted at different end strengths, and to share the details of these assessments with other stakeholders.

In a similar vein, the QDRs were consistently criticized for not focusing sufficient attention on the long-run implications of the active-reserve mix—for example, the decision to shift from relying on the reserves as a strategic reserve to treating them as an operational reserve.

- *Recommendation*: Before or during the next Defense Strategy Review, it will be important for the Army to address the active-reserve mix that will best support the strategy in the emerging post-war environment, including the rotational depth and readiness requirements that can meet the demands of steady-state and contingency response operations.

The costs associated with Army major acquisition programs continued to grow over the period examined, as a result of both procurement of increasingly sophisticated (and therefore expensive) systems and difficulties in implementing acquisition reforms that might have helped to reduce the cost growth in major acquisition programs.

- *Recommendation*: Now facing increasingly scarce resources and a future "bow wave" in procurement, the Army should focus attention on the sort of high-low mix in platforms and capabilities that will best meet operational requirements at an affordable cost over the longer term.

Finally, our review suggests that over time, and quite properly in light of the wars being fought in Afghanistan, Iraq, and elsewhere, the QDRs became increasingly focused on shorter-term planning considerations at the expense of considering longer-term threats and transformation. Nonetheless, longer-term challenges continue to grow.

- *Recommendation*: As the Army achieves a reset of the force, in the next defense review, more consideration should be given to future challenges risk and longer-term capability development and transformation requirements.

Concluding Thoughts

The period of study thus ends much as it began, with an increasingly apparent strategy-forces-resources gap that will need to be closed. As in 2001, the defense strategy, program, and budget in 2015 appear to be out of balance; a low- to moderate-risk strategy to ensure continued U.S. leadership in the presence of expansive commitments and growing threats requires greater defense capabilities and resources than are currently being afforded. Also as in 2001, near-term considerations have eclipsed planning for future threats and capabilities.

As defense needs and strategies continue to evolve, it will be left to civilian and military senior leaders in DoD to estimate the funding levels that are needed to ensure low to moderate risk in the execution of the strategy. And it will be left to the White House and Congress to agree on a stable level of defense funding and to determine how best to pay that bill while also addressing pressing domestic requirements and achieving deficit reduction targets.

While it cannot be entirely ruled out, it remains doubtful to us that policymakers would choose to trim the United States' aims and role in the world and accept the resulting risks to U.S. leadership and global security. Rather, questions going forward will most likely revolve around the adequacy of the forces to support the strategy and the budgets that are needed to support the forces in the near, mid-, and long terms.

References

Belasco, Amy, *The Cost of Iraq, Afghanistan, and Other Global War on Terror Operations Since 9/11*, Washington, D.C.: Congressional Research Service, December 8, 2014.

Bonds, Timothy M., Eric V. Larson, Derek Eaton, and Richard E. Darilek, *Strategy-Policy Mismatch: How the U.S. Army Can Help Close Gaps in Countering Weapons of Mass Destruction*, Santa Monica, Calif.: RAND Corporation, RR-541-RC, 2014. As of November 22, 2016: http://www.rand.org/pubs/research_reports/RR541.html

DoD—*See* U.S. Department of Defense.

Garamone, Jim, "Army Chief 'Adamantly Opposes' Added End Strength," *American Forces Press Service*, January 28, 2004.

Gates, Robert M., "A Balanced Strategy: Reprogramming the Pentagon for a New Age," *Foreign Affairs*, January/February 2009.

Gunzinger, Mark, *Shaping America's Future Military: Toward a New Force Planning Construct*, Washington, D.C.: Center for Strategic and Budgetary Assessments, 2013.

House Armed Services Committee, "Chairman McKeon Rejects QDR," press release, Washington, D.C., March 4, 2014.

Larson, Eric V., Derek Eaton, Michael E. Linick, John E. Peters, Agnes Gereben Schaefer, Keith Walters, Stephanie Young, H. G. Massey, and Michelle Darrah Ziegler, *Defense Planning in a Time of Conflict: A Comparative Analysis of the 2001–2014 Quadrennial Defense Reviews, and Implications for the Army*, Santa Monica, Calif.: RAND Corporation, RR-1309-A, 2018. As of January 12, 2018: http://www.rand.org/pubs/research_reports/RR1309.html

Larson, Eric V., David T. Orletsky, and Kristin J. Leuschner, *Defense Planning in a Decade of Change: Lessons from the Base Force, Bottom-Up Review, and Quadrennial Defense Review*, Santa Monica, Calif.: RAND Corporation, MR-1387-AF, 2001. As of November 22, 2016: http://www.rand.org/pubs/monograph_reports/MR1387.html

Odierno, Raymond T., "Total Force Policy for the U.S. Army," statement before the Senate Armed Services Committee, Washington, D.C., April 8, 2014.

Office of the Under Secretary of Defense (Comptroller), "DoD Budget Request," web page, various years. As of December 14, 2015: http://comptroller.defense.gov/budgetmaterials.aspx

———, *National Defense Budget Estimates for FY 2015*, Washington, D.C., April 2014.

OUSD (Comptroller)—*See* Office of the Under Secretary of Defense (Comptroller).

Sherman, Jason, "Work Grabs Reins of Analysis Effort Pivotal to Strategy, Budget Decisions," *Inside Defense*, November 26, 2014.

United States Code, Title 10, Section 153, Chairman: Functions, 2010.

United States Code, Title 50, Section 3043, Annual National Security Strategy Report, 2013.

U.S. Department of Defense, *Report of the Quadrennial Defense Review*, Washington, D.C., May 1997.

———, *Quadrennial Defense Review Report*, Washington, D.C., September 30, 2001.

———, *Data Collection, Development, and Management in Support of Strategic Analysis*, Washington, D.C., DoD Directive 8260.1, December 6, 2002.

———, *Quadrennial Defense Review Report*, Washington, D.C., February 6, 2006.

———, *Support for Strategic Analysis*, Washington, D.C., DoD Instruction 8260.01, January 11, 2007.

———, *Quadrennial Defense Review Report*, Washington, D.C., February 2010.

———, *Support for Strategic Analysis (SSA)*, Washington, D.C., DoD Directive 8260.05, July 7, 2011.

———, *Quadrennial Defense Review Report*, Washington, D.C., March 2014a.

———, "News Release: DoD Releases Fiscal 2015 Budget Proposal and 2014 QDR," Washington, D.C., March 4, 2014b.

U.S. House of Representatives, *The 2010 Quadrennial Defense Review: Hearing Before the Committee on Armed Services*, Washington, D.C., February 4, 2010.

———, *The 2014 Quadrennial Defense Review: Hearing Before the Committee on Armed Services*, Washington, D.C., April 3, 2014.